# TREATS

## just great recipes

GENERAL INFORMATION

The level of difficulty of the recipes in this book
is expressed as a number from 1 (simple) to 3 (difficult).

# potatoes

McRae Books

SERVES 4

PREPARATION 10 min

COOKING 20 min

DIFFICULTY level 1

# Creamy Potato
## and leek soup

Place the potatoes, leeks, and chives in a large saucepan over medium heat. Add the stock and bring to a boil. Season with salt and pepper. Cover and cook until the potatoes are tender, 15 minutes. • Chop in a food processor until smooth. • Return the soup to the saucepan over low heat. Add the cream and mix well. Heat the soup, stirring continuously, without letting it boil. • Garnish with chives and serve hot.

1 lb (500 g) starchy (baking) potatoes, peeled and cut into small cubes

4 leeks, cleaned and sliced

3 tablespoons finely chopped chives, + extra, to garnish

4 cups (1 liter) vegetable stock, (homemade or bouillon cube), boiling

Salt and freshly ground black pepper

1/2 cup (125 ml) heavy (double) cream

SERVES 4
PREPARATION 15 min
COOKING 40 min
DIFFICULTY level 1

# Creamy Potato
## and herb soup

Melt 1 tablespoon of butter in a large saucepan over low heat. Add the onion, celery, parsley, basil, and chervil. Cover and simmer until the onion begins to soften, about 5 minutes. • Add the water and potatoes. Season with salt and bring to a boil. Cover and simmer until the potatoes begin to break down, about 30 minutes. • Remove from the heat and chop in a food processor until smooth. • Whip the cream in a small bowl until thick. • Return the soup to the saucepan over low heat. Stir in the remaining butter. • Ladle the soup into soup bowls. Top each bowl with cream. Season with pepper. Garnish with basil and serve hot.

1/4 cup (60 g) butter
1 large onion, chopped
4 oz (125 g) celery leaves, chopped
2 tablespoons finely chopped parsley
1 tablespoon finely chopped basil
1 tablespoon finely chopped chervil
4 cups (1 liter) boiling water
2 lb (1 kg) starchy (baking) potatoes, peeled and cut into small cubes
Salt
1/2 cup (125 ml) heavy (double) cream
Freshly ground black pepper
Sprigs of basil, to garnish

SERVES 4–6

PREPARATION 30 min

COOKING 35 min

DIFFICULTY level 1

# Potato Salad
## with tomatoes and onion

Cook the potatoes in a large pot of salted boiling water until tender, 20–25 minutes. Drain well and let cool slightly. Slip off their skins. Cut into ¼-inch (5-mm) thick slices. • Preheat the oven to 400°F (200°C/gas 6). • Grease a large baking pan and layer the potatoes into it. Sprinkle with the chopped coriander, parsley, and basil. Drizzle with 2 tablespoons of the oil. • Bake until the potatoes are lightly browned, about 10 minutes. Remove from the oven and let cool slightly. • Heat 2 tablespoons of the oil in a large frying pan over medium heat. • Add the garlic and sauté until pale golden brown, about 2 minutes. Add the tomatoes and sauté for 3 minutes. Remove from the heat. • Beat together the remaining oil with the vinegar in a small bowl. Season with salt and pepper. • Cover the potatoes with the tomatoes and onion rings. Drizzle with the dressing. Season with pepper, garnish with the herbs, and serve.

2 lb (1 kg) waxy (boiling) potatoes
2 tablespoons finely chopped coriander,
  + sprigs to garnish
2 tablespoons finely chopped parsley,
  + sprigs to garnish
2 tablespoons finely chopped basil,
  + leaves to garnish
½ cup (125 ml) extra-virgin olive oil
1 clove garlic, finely chopped
1 lb (500 g) ripe tomatoes,
  peeled and chopped
1 large red onion, thinly sliced
2 tablespoons white wine vinegar
Salt and freshly ground black pepper

SERVES 4

PREPARATION 15 min + 30 min to cool

COOKING 15–20 min

DIFFICULTY level 1

# Potato Salad
## with scallions and herbs

Cook the potatoes in a large pot of salted boiling water until tender, 15–20 minutes. • Drain well and transfer to a salad bowl. Let cool for 30 minutes. • Add the green onions. • Beat the oil ad the vinegar in a small bowl. Season with salt and pepper. • Drizzle the dressing over the salad. Add the garlic, mint, and parsley. Toss gently and serve.

1½ lb (750 g) new potatoes, larger ones cut in half
6 scallions (green onions), sliced
¼ cup (40 ml) extra-virgin olive oil
1–2 tablespoons red wine vinegar
Salt and freshly ground black pepper
1 clove garlic, finely chopped
2 tablespoons finely chopped mint
2 tablespoons finely chopped parsley

SERVES 4–6

PREPARATION 15 min

COOKING 20–25 min

DIFFICULTY level 1

# Potato Salad
## with broccoli

Cook the potatoes in a large pot of salted boiling water until tender, 20–25 minutes. • Drain and let cool slightly. Cut potatoes into small cubes. Place in a large salad bowl. • While the potatoes are cooking, boil the broccoli in a large pot of salted boiling water until just tender, about 5 minutes. • Drain well and add to the salad bowl. Add the onion. • Beat together the oil, vinegar, garlic, chives, capers, and parsley in a small bowl with a fork. Season with salt and pepper. • Drizzle the dressing over the salad and serve while still warm.

4 large waxy (boiling) potatoes, peeled
1½ lb (750 g) broccoli florets
1 small red onion, chopped
¼ cup (60 ml) extra-virgin olive oil
1–2 tablespoons white wine vinegar
1 clove garlic, finely chopped
2 tablespoons finely chopped chives
1 tablespoon capers preserved in brine, rinsed and drained
4 tablespoons finely chopped parsley
Salt and freshly ground black pepper

SERVES 4

PREPARATION 20 min

COOKING 50 min

DIFFICULTY level 2

# Potato Omelets
## with herbs and cream cheese

Cook the potatoes in a large pot of salted boiling water until tender, 20–25 minutes. • Drain and let cool slightly. Cut into ½-inch (1-cm) cubes. • Melt half the butter in a large frying pan over medium-high heat. Add the potatoes and sauté until lightly browned, 3–4 minutes. Remove from the heat and let cool slightly. • Add the chives, coriander, marjoram, and chervil, and toss gently • Beat the eggs in a large bowl. Season with salt and pepper. • Heat a little of the remaining butter in an 8-inch (20-cm) nonstick frying pan. • Pour a quarter of the egg mixture into the pan and cook on both sides until the egg is almost set, about 5 minutes. • Spread each omelet with a quarter of the cheese. Sprinkle with a quarter of the potato and herb mixture. • Fold the omelets over the filling. • Serve hot.

12 oz (350 g) waxy (boiling) potatoes, peeled
¼ cup (60 g) butter
2 tablespoons finely chopped chives
1 tablespoon finely chopped coriander
1 tablespoon finely chopped marjoram
1 tablespoon finely chopped chervil
8 large eggs
Salt and freshly ground black pepper
4 oz (125 g) cream cheese or mascarpone, at room temperature

# Potato Salad
## with olives, celery, and tomatoes

Cook the potatoes in a large pot of salted boiling water until tender, 15–20 minutes. Drain well and let cool slightly. • Place the olives in a large salad bowl. Add the basil, garlic, and vinegar, and toss well. • Add the potatoes to the salad bowl. • Toss gently and let cool completely. • Add the celery and tomatoes. Drizzle with the oil and season with salt. • Toss gently and serve.

2 lb (1 kg) small new potatoes, larger ones cut in half
1 cup (100 g) green olives, pitted
1 cup (100 g) black olives, pitted
2 tablespoons finely chopped basil
1 clove garlic, finely chopped
1 tablespoon white wine vinegar
1 small head of celery, sliced
16 cherry tomatoes, halved
$1/4$ cup (60 ml) extra-virgin olive oil
Salt

# Potato Bake

## with cheese and eggs

Preheat the oven to 350°F (180°C/gas 4). • Grease a large ovenproof dish. • Parboil the potatoes in a large pot of salted boiling water for 2 minutes. Drain well. • Arrange a layer of potatoes in the dish. Sprinkle with a little of the cheese and some of the thyme. Drizzle with oil and season with salt and pepper. Add another layer of potatoes and repeat until all the potatoes are in the dish. Sprinkle with the remaining thyme and finish with a layer of cheese. Drizzle with a little more oil. • Bake until the potatoes are tender, 20–25 minutes. • Preheat a broiler (grill) on a high setting. Place the potatoes under the broiler and cook until browned, 2–3 minutes. • Divide the potato among 4 individual serving dishes. • Heat the remaining oil in a large frying pan over medium heat. Add the garlic and eggs and fry until cooked, about 5 minutes. • Top each serving with an egg. Sprinkle with the remaining cheese and season with pepper. Serve hot.

1½ lb (750 g) waxy potatoes, peeled and thinly sliced

8 oz (250 g) mild Pecorino or other mild firm cheese, coarsely grated

2 tablespoons finely chopped thyme

⅓ cup (90 ml) extra-virgin olive oil

Salt and freshly ground black pepper

1 clove garlic, lightly crushed but whole

4 large eggs

Sprigs of thyme, to garnish

# Sautéed Potatoes
## with shrimp

Steam the potatoes until just cooked, about 15 minutes. • Heat the oil and butter in a large frying pan over medium heat. Add the garlic and sauté until pale gold, 2–3 minutes. • Add the scallions and shrimp. Turn the heat up to high and add the potatoes. Sauté for 5 minutes. • Season with salt and the peppercorns. Cook over low heat for 2 minutes. • Sprinkle with chives and serve hot.

1 lb (500 g) small new potatoes, larger ones cut in half

2 tablespoons extra-virgin olive oil

1 tablespoon butter

1 clove garlic, finely chopped

8 scallions (green onions), sliced

14 oz (400 g) fresh shrimp (prawn) tails, shelled and deveined

Salt

$1/2$ teaspoon black peppercorns, lightly crushed

2 tablespoons finely chopped chives

SERVES 4–6

PREPARATION 15 min

COOKING 35 min

DIFFICULTY level 1

# Creamy Potato
## purée with carrots and celery

Cook the potatoes in a large pot of salted boiling water until tender, 20–25 minutes. Drain and let cool slightly. • Add the milk and butter and mash in the pot until smooth. • Chop the celery, carrots, garlic, and oil in a food processor until smooth (reserve a few pieces of the vegetables to garnish). Season with salt and pepper. • Stir the vegetable purée and eggs into the potatoes until well incorporated. • Place the pot over medium heat and stir until the mixture begins to come away from the sides of the pan, 5–10 minutes. • Garnish with the reserved celery and carrot and serve hot.

1½ lb (750 g) starchy (baking) potatoes, peeled
½ cup (125 ml) milk
1 tablespoon butter
4 oz (125 g) celery, chopped
3 large carrots, chopped
1 clove garlic, chopped
2 tablespoons extra-virgin olive oil
Salt and freshly ground black pepper
2 large eggs, lightly beaten

# New Potatoes
## in egg sauce

Steam the potatoes in their skins until tender, 15–20 minutes. Remove from the heat and let cool slightly. • Beat the egg yolks with the cream and Parmesan in a large bowl. Season with salt and pepper. • Add the potatoes and mix well. • Melt the butter in a large frying pan over medium heat. Add the bacon and sauté until crisp and lightly browned, about 5 minutes. • Add the potato mixture and sauté until the sauce thickens, about 2 minutes. • Add the chives and season with pepper. Serve hot.

2 lb (1 kg) small new potatoes, larger ones cut in half
2 large egg yolks
1/3 cup (90 ml) heavy (double) cream
1/2 cup (60 g) freshly grated Parmesan
Salt and freshly ground black pepper
3 tablespoons butter
5 oz (150 g) bacon, chopped
3 tablespoons finely chopped chives

SERVES 4–6

PREPARATION 15 min

COOKING 45 min

DIFFICULTY level 1

# Potato Caponata

Heat the olive oil in a large frying pan over medium heat. Fry the potatoes until lightly browned, 5–10 minutes. • Remove from the pan using a slotted spoon and drain on paper towels. • Heat the extra-virgin olive oil in a large frying pan over medium heat. Add the onions and celery. Sauté until they begin to soften, 3–4 minutes. • Add the potatoes and mix well. Add the pine nuts, almonds, raisins, olives, pear, capers, sugar, and vinegar. Season with salt. Mix gently and then add the tomato and oregano. Cover and simmer over low heat until the sauce is thick and the potatoes are tender, about 25 minutes. • Garnish with chile pepper and serve hot or at room temperature.

$^1/_2$ cup (125 ml) olive oil, for frying
1$^1/_2$ lb (750 g) waxy (boiling) potatoes, peeled and cut into small cubes
3 tablespoons extra-virgin olive oil
1 large onion, chopped
2 celery sticks, chopped
Generous $^1/_2$ cup (100 g) pine nuts
$^2/_3$ cup (100 g) blanched almonds, coarsely chopped
Generous $^1/_2$ cup (100 g) raisins
1 cup (100 g) green olives
1 large pear, peeled, cored, and cut into small cubes
1 tablespoon capers, rinsed
1 tablespoon sugar
1 tablespoon white wine vinegar
Salt
$^1/_2$ cup (125 g) canned tomatoes
1 tablespoon finely chopped oregano
1 red chile pepper, seeded and sliced

# Potatoes

## with pancetta in white wine

Steam the potatoes in their skins for 10 minutes. • Melt the butter in a large frying pan over low heat. Add the onion, sugar, and bay leaves and sauté until the onion is transparent, 4–5 minutes. Add a little water if the mixture begins to stick to the pan. • Add the wine and cook until it evaporates, 2–3 minutes. • Sauté the pancetta in a small nonstick frying pan over medium heat until crisp, 3–4 minutes. • Add the potatoes and pancetta to the pan with the onions. Season with salt and pepper. Add the stock and simmer over medium heat until the potatoes are tender, about 10 minutes. • Remove from the heat. Cover and let rest for 5 minutes. Discard the bay leaves and serve hot.

1½ lb 1 (750 g) small red potatoes, scrubbed and cut into wedges

2 tablespoons butter

1 large onion, chopped

1 teaspoon sugar

2 bay leaves

Generous ⅓ cup (100 ml) dry white wine

5 oz (150 g) pancetta or bacon, diced

Salt and freshly ground black pepper

Generous ⅓ cup (100 ml) beef stock (homemade or bouillon cube)

# Potatoes
## with balsamic dressing

Steam the potatoes in their skins until tender, 15–20 minutes. Let cool slightly and slip off their skins. • Beat the oil and vinegar in a small bowl. Season with salt and pepper. • Transfer the potatoes to a serving dish. • Drizzle with the dressing. Sprinkle with mint and serve at once.

1 lb (500 g) new potatoes, halved
1/4 cup (60 ml) extra-virgin olive oil
2 tablespoons balsamic vinegar
Salt and freshly ground black pepper
2 tablespoons finely chopped mint

SERVES 4–6

PREPARATION 45 min

COOKING 1 h

DIFFICULTY level 2

# Potato Gnocchi
## gratin with leeks

Gnocchi: Cook the potatoes in a large pot of salted boiling water until tender, 20–25 minutes. Drain and let cool slightly. • Slip off their skins and mash until smooth. • Gradually stir in the egg yolks and enough of the flour to obtain a soft but smooth dough that is just a little sticky. • Take a piece of dough and roll it on a lightly floured work surface into a "sausage" about 1/2 inch (1 cm) in diameter. Cut into pieces about 1 inch (2.5 cm) long. Repeat with all the dough. • To give the gnocchi their special grooves, twist them around the tines of a fork. • Place the gnocchi on a lightly floured clean cloth well spaced so they do not stick together. • Set a large pot of salted water to boil. The gnocchi should be cooked in batches. Lower the first batch (20–24 gnocchi) gently into the boiling water. After a few minutes they will rise to the surface. Simmer for 1 minute, then scoop out with a slotted spoon. Place on a heated dish. Repeat until all the gnocchi are cooked. • Sauce: Preheat the oven to 400°F (200°C/gas 6). • Butter 1 large or 4–6 individual ovenproof baking dishes. • Beat the cream and cornstarch in a small bowl. • Melt the butter in a large frying pan over medium heat. Add the leeks and sauté until they begin to soften, 3–4 minutes. • Add 3 tablespoons of water and cook until the leeks are tender, about 5 minutes. • Add the cognac and cook over high heat until it evaporates, 2–3 minutes. • Lower the heat and add the cream and cornstarch. Mix well to prevent lumps forming. Cook until thickened, 5 minutes. Add the nutmeg and season with salt and pepper. • Place the cooked gnocchi in the prepared baking dish(es). Spoon the leek sauce over the top. Sprinkle with Parmesan. • Bake until lightly browned, 5–10 minutes. • Garnish with basil and serve hot.

Gnocchi
2 lb (1 kg) starchy (baking) potatoes
2 large egg yolks
2 cups (300 g) all-purpose (plain) flour

Sauce
1 1/4 cups (300 ml) heavy (double) cream
1 tablespoon cornstarch (cornflour)
2 tablespoons butter
5 small leeks, thinly sliced
2 tablespoons cognac
1/4 teaspoon freshly grated nutmeg
Salt and freshly ground black pepper
3/4 cup (90 g) freshly grated Parmesan
Sprigs of basil, to garnish

SERVES 4–6

PREPARATION 15 min + time to make gnocchi

COOKING 30 min

DIFFICULTY level 2

# Potato Gnocchi
## with vegetable sauce

Heat the oil in a large frying pan over medium heat. Add the garlic and sauté until pale gold, 2–3 minutes. • Add the bell pepper and beans. Sauté until softened, 5–10 minutes. • Add the tomatoes and water and season with salt and pepper. Lower the heat, cover, and simmer until the vegetables are tender and cooked, 10–15 minutes. Stir in the parsley and oregano. • Cook the gnocchi in small batches in a large pot of salted boiling water until they rise to the surface. Let simmer for 1 minute then scoop out with a slotted spoon. Place on a heated dish while you finish cooking the gnocchi. • Add the gnocchi to the frying pan with the sauce. Sauté over high heat for 1 minute. Serve hot.

¼ cup (60 ml) extra-virgin olive oil
1 clove garlic, finely chopped
1 large yellow bell pepper (capsicum), seeded and chopped
5 oz (150 g) green beans, cut into short sections
1 lb (500 g) ripe tomatoes, peeled and chopped
⅓ cup (90 ml) water
Salt and freshly ground black pepper
2 tablespoons finely chopped parsley
1 tablespoon finely chopped oregano
2 lb (1 kg) potato gnocchi (storebought or homemade — see page 22)

# Potato Gnocchi

## with zucchini, carrots, and peas

Melt the butter in a large frying pan over medium heat. Add the onion and sauté until transparent, 3–4 minutes. • Add the carrots, zucchini, and peas. Sauté until the vegetables begin to soften, about 5 minutes. • Add the water, cover, and simmer until the vegetables are tender, about 10 minutes. Season with salt and pepper. • Cook the gnocchi in small batches in a large pot of salted boiling water until they rise to the surface. Let simmer for 1 minute then scoop out with a slotted spoon. Place on a heated dish and finish cooking all the gnocchi. • Add the gnocchi to the frying pan with the sauce. Sauté over high heat for 1 minute. • Sprinkle with the cheese and serve hot.

2 tablespoons butter
1 large onion, finely chopped
2 large carrots, cut into small cubes
2 large zucchini (courgettes),
    cut into small cubes
1 cup (150 g) frozen peas
$1/3$ cup (90 ml) water
Salt and freshly ground black pepper
2 lb (1 kg) potato gnocchi (storebought
    or homemade — see page 22)
$1/2$ cup (60 g) freshly grated Emmental
    or other firm, mild cheese

SERVES 4–6

PREPARATION 30 min

COOKING 45 min

DIFFICULTY level 2

# Brown Gnocchi

## with cheese fondue sauce

Place the cheese in a bowl and cover with the milk. Leave to soak until you are ready to prepare the fondue sauce. • Cook the potatoes in a large pot of salted boiling water until tender, 20–25 minutes. Drain and mash until smooth. • Place the potato purée in a large bowl. Gradually stir both flours. Season with salt and pepper. Mix well to make a smooth dough. • Knead the dough on a lightly floured work surface until smooth and elastic, 3–4 minutes. • Roll the dough into long "sausages" about 3/4 inch (2 cm) in diameter. Cut into pieces about 1 inch (2.5 cm) long. Repeat with all the dough. • Place the gnocchi on a lightly floured clean cloth well spaced so they do not stick together. • Place the cheese and 3 tablespoons of the milk in a double boiler over barely simmering water. Add the butter and stir until the cheese has melted, about 5 minutes. • Add the egg yolks one at a time, mixing well after each addition. • Cook, stirring constantly, until the sauce is thick, about 5 minutes. Season with salt and pepper. • Cook the gnocchi in small batches in a large pot of salted boiling water until they rise to the surface. Let simmer for 1 minute then scoop out with a slotted spoon. Place on a heated dish while you finish cooking the gnocchi. • Place in a large heated serving bowl and pour the cheese fondue sauce over the top. Mix gently and serve hot.

14 oz (400 g) Fontina or other mild cheese suitable for melting, sliced
2/3 cup (150 ml) milk
2 lb (1 kg) starchy (baking) potatoes
2/3 cup (100 g) all-purpose (plain) flour
2/3 cup (100 g) buckwheat flour
Salt and freshly ground black pepper
1 tablespoon butter
2 large egg yolks, lightly beaten

SERVES 4

PREPARATION 40 min

COOKING 50 min

DIFFICULTY level 3

# Potato Ravioli

## with zucchini sauce

Cook the potatoes in a large pot of salted boiling water until tender, 20–25 minutes. Drain well and transfer to a large bowl. • Purée the potatoes using a potato ricer and let cool. • Add the flour and egg yolks. Season with salt and mix well to make a smooth dough. • Turn the dough out onto a lightly floured work surface and knead until smooth and elastic, 5 minutes. • Roll out the dough on a lightly floured work surface until 1/4 inch (5 mm) thick. Cut into 2-inch (5-cm) disks using a glass or cookie cutter. • Beat the goat cheese and Parmesan with a fork in a small bowl until smooth. • Place the marble-size balls of this mixture on half of the disks of pasta. • Brush the edges of these disks with the beaten egg white. Cover with the remaining disks and press gently around the edges of each ravioli to seal. • Arrange the ravioli on a lightly floured plate. • Zucchini Sauce: Heat the oil in a large frying pan over medium heat. Add the shallot and sauté until tender, 3–4 minutes. • Add the zucchini and stock. Cover and simmer until the zucchini are very tender, about 10 minutes. • Reserve 2–3 tablespoons of the zucchini, and chop the rest in a food processor until smooth. • Cook the ravioli in small batches in a large pot of salted boiling water until al dente, 3–4 minutes. • Transfer to a heated serving dish using a slotted spoon. Spoon the zucchini sauce over the top. Garnish with the reserved zucchini and serve hot.

Ravioli

1 lb (500 g) starchy (baking) potatoes, peeled

1 1/3 cups (200 g) all-purpose (plain) flour

2 large egg yolks, lightly beaten

Salt

4 oz (125 g) soft creamy goat cheese

1 tablespoon freshly grated Parmesan

1 large egg white, lightly beaten

Zucchini Sauce

1/4 cup (60 ml) extra-virgin olive oil

1 shallot, finely chopped

3 large zucchini/courgettes, sliced

Generous 3/4 cup (200 ml) vegetable stock, (homemade or bouillon cube), boiling

Small bunch fresh basil

SERVES 4–6

PREPARATION 15 min

COOKING 1 h

DIFFICULTY level 1

# Baked Potato

## with cabbage and cumin

Cook the potatoes in a large pot of salted boiling water until tender, 20–25 minutes. Drain well. • Mash two-thirds of the potatoes. Cut the remaining potatoes into bite-size pieces. • Place the potatoes in a large bowl. • Preheat the oven to 350°F (180°C/gas 4). • Heat the oil in a large frying pan over medium heat. Add the garlic and cabbage and sauté until the cabbage is tender, 10–15 minutes. • Add the cabbage to the potatoes and mix gently. Add the eggs, mozzarella, half the cumin, and Parmesan. Season with salt and pepper. Mix well. • Grease a 10-inch (25-cm) baking pan. • Spoon the mixture into the pan and level the surface with the back of a spoon. Sprinkle with the remaining cumin seeds. • Bake until lightly browned, 35–40 minutes. • Serve hot.

2 lb (1 kg) starchy (baking) potatoes, peeled
3 tablespoons extra-virgin olive oil
2 cloves garlic, finely chopped
12 oz (350 g) savoy cabbage, coarsely chopped
3 large eggs, lightly beaten
5 oz (150 g) mozzarella, cut into small cubes
1 teaspoon cumin seeds
$\frac{1}{2}$ cup (60 g) freshly grated Parmesan
Salt and freshly ground black pepper

# Baked Potatoes
## with mushrooms

Preheat the oven to 375°F (190°C/gas 5). • Grease a large oven-proof dish. • Melt two-thirds of the butter in a small saucepan over medium heat. Stir in the flour. Remove from the heat and add a little milk. Mix well. Add the remaining milk. Return to the heat and cook, stirring constantly, until thick and creamy, 5–7 minutes. Season with salt and pepper and remove from the heat. • Stir in the Parmesan. • Heat the oil in a large frying pan over medium heat. Add the potatoes and sauté for 5 minutes. • Add the mushrooms and sauté for 5 minutes. Season with salt and pepper. • Stir the potatoes and mushrooms into the cream sauce. Place in the prepared dish and dot with the remaining butter. Sprinkle with the parsley. • Bake until the potatoes are tender, 20–25 minutes. Serve hot.

1/3 cup (90 g) butter
1/4 cup (30 g) all-purpose (plain) flour
2 cups (500 ml) milk
Salt and freshly ground black pepper
1/4 cup (30 g) freshly grated Parmesan
2 tablespoons extra-virgin olive oil
1 lb (500 g) starchy (baking) potatoes, peeled and thinly sliced
5 oz (150 g) mixed frozen mushrooms
2 tablespoons finely chopped parsley

31

# Baked Potato
## layer cake

Cook the potatoes in a large pot of salted boiling water until tender, 20–25 minutes. • Drain well and mash until smooth. • Preheat the oven to 375°F (190°C/gas 5). • Line a 9-inch (23-cm) baking pan with waxed paper. • Cook the mixed vegetables in a large pot of salted boiling water until tender, 5–10 minutes. Drain well. • Mix the potato, Parmesan, Cheddar, milk, cream, 4 tablespoons of butter, the eggs, and nutmeg in a large bowl. Season with salt and pepper. Add the mixed vegetables and stir well. • Spoon half the mixture into the prepared pan. Cover with the ham and top with the remaining vegetable mixture. Sprinkle with bread crumbs and drizzle with the remaining butter. • Bake until browned, 45–50 minutes. Serve hot or at room temperature.

2 lb (1 kg) starchy (baking) potatoes, peeled

3 cups (500 g) fresh or frozen mixed vegetables, cut in small cubes

1/2 cup (60 g) freshly grated Parmesan

4 oz (125 g) Cheddar or other mild firm cheese, cut into small cubes

Generous 1/3 cup (100 ml) milk

1/2 cup (125 ml) heavy (double) cream

1/3 cup (90 g) butter, melted

4 large eggs, lightly beaten

1/2 teaspoon freshly grated nutmeg

Salt and freshly ground black pepper

4 oz (125 g) ham, sliced

4–6 tablespoons fine dry bread crumbs

# Baked Potatoes
## with bacon and cabbage

Preheat the oven to 400°F (200°C/gas 6). • Heat the oil in a large frying pan over medium heat. Add one-third of the onion and sauté until it begins to soften, 2–3 minutes. • Add the cabbage and sauté until tender, about 10 minutes. • Put the remaining onion and the water into a small saucepan and bring to a boil over medium heat. Cook until the onion is tender, 3–5 minutes. Drain, reserving the cooking juices. Discard the boiled onion or use it in another recipe. • Grease a large ovenproof dish. • Spoon a layer of cabbage into the dish. Cover with a layer of potatoes and season with salt. Add a layer of bacon and then a layer of tomatoes. Add another layer of cabbage and continue, alternating layers, until all the ingredients are in the dish. Finish with a layer of potatoes. Season with salt and pepper. • Drizzle with the reserved cooking juices. Sprinkle with Parmesan. • Bake for 20 minutes. Cover with aluminum foil and bake until the potatoes are tender, about 20 minutes. Remove the foil and bake until lightly browned, 5 minutes. • Serve hot.

1/4 cup (60 ml) extra-virgin olive oil
3 small onions, chopped
14 oz (400 g) savoy cabbage, shredded
1 cup (250 ml) water
1 1/2 lb (750 g) starchy (baking) potatoes, thinly sliced
Salt
5 oz (150 g) bacon, sliced into ribbons
4 large ripe tomatoes, sliced
Freshly ground black pepper
Generous 3/4 cup (100 g) freshly grated Parmesan

# Potato Frittata

## with peas and mint

Cook the potatoes in a large pot of salted boiling water until tender, 20–25 minutes. Drain well. • Cook the peas in a medium pot of salted boiling water until tender, about 5 minutes. Drain well. • Preheat the oven to 350°F (180°C/gas 4). • Grease a 9-inch (23-cm) baking pan. • Cut the potatoes into small cubes. • Beat the eggs in a large bowl. Season with salt and pepper. Add the onions, peas, potatoes, and mint and mix well. • Spoon the mixture into the prepared pan. Bake until set and lightly browned, about 25 minutes. • Garnish with the mint, if liked, and serve hot.

14 oz (400 g) waxy (boiling) potatoes, peeled

1½ cups (250 g) fresh or frozen peas

6 large eggs

Salt and freshly ground black pepper

2 medium onions, finely chopped

1 tablespoon finely chopped mint, + whole sprigs, to garnish (optional)

SERVES 4–6

PREPARATION 15 min

COOKING 55 min

DIFFICULTY level 2

# Potato Soufflé

Preheat the oven to 350°F (180°C/gas 4). • Grease a 1-quart (1-liter) soufflé dish. • Cook the potatoes in a large pot of salted boiling water until tender, 20–25 minutes. • Drain and mash in a large bowl using a potato ricer. • Add the cream and season with salt and pepper. Mix well. Add the egg yolks and mix well. • Beat the egg whites in a large bowl until stiff. Gently fold into the potato mixture. • Spoon the mixture into the soufflé dish. • Bake for 15 minutes. Increase the oven temperature to 375°F (190°C/gas 5). Bake until well risen and golden brown, about 15 minutes. • Serve at once.

$1^1/_2$ lb (750 g) starchy (baking) potatoes, peeled
$^1/_3$ cup (90 ml) heavy (double) cream
Salt and freshly ground black pepper
4 large eggs, separated

SERVES 4

PREPARATION 30 min + 30 min to cool

COOKING 50 min

DIFFICULTY level 3

# Potato Roulade

## with spinach and ricotta

Cook the potatoes in a large pot of salted boiling water until tender, 20–25 minutes. • Drain and mash in a large bowl. • Cook the spinach in salted boiling until tender, 4–5 minutes. Drain well and chop finely. • Mix the spinach, ricotta, 1 egg yolk, half the Parmesan, and the nutmeg in a bowl. Season with salt and pepper. • Add the remaining egg yolk, remaining Parmesan, the flour, and a pinch of salt to the bowl with the potatoes and mix well. • Roll out the potato mixture on a sheet of parchment paper to 1/4 inch (5 mm) thick. • Spread the spinach mixture over the potato, leaving a 1-inch (2.5-cm) border around the edges. • Carefully roll up the roulade using the parchment paper to help you. Wrap the roulade securely in the paper and seal the ends, tying with kitchen string. • Put the roulade into a large casserole and cover with boiling water. • Simmer gently for 20 minutes. Remove from the heat and drain. Let the roulade cool completely before unwrapping it. • Melt the butter with the sage in a small saucepan. Unwrap and slice the roulade. Arrange on a serving dish. Drizzle with the butter and serve.

1 lb (500 g) starchy (baking) potatoes, peeled
12 oz (350 g) fresh spinach, well washed
5 oz (150 g) ricotta cheese, drained
2 large egg yolks, lightly beaten
1/2 cup (60 g) freshly grated Parmesan
1/4 teaspoon freshly grated nutmeg
Salt and freshly ground black pepper
2/3 cup (100 g) fine polenta (stoneground corn)
1/4 cup (60 g) butter
6 sage leaves

# Potato Pancake

## cake with mushrooms

Cook the potatoes in a large pot of salted boiling water until tender, 20–25 minutes. • Drain and mash in a large bowl using a potato ricer. Let cool. • Add the eggs, 1/3 cup (50 g) of the flour and 2/3 cup (150 ml) of the milk. Season with salt and pepper and mix well. Chill in the refrigerator for 10 minutes. • Melt 3 tablespoons of the butter in a large saucepan over medium heat. Add the remaining flour and mix well. Remove from the heat and add a little of the milk. Mix well. Add the remaining milk and mix well. • Return to the heat and cook, stirring constantly, until the thick and creamy, 7–10 minutes. Season with salt and pepper and remove from the heat. • Stir in the Parmesan. • Heat the oil in a large frying pan over medium heat. Add the mushrooms and sauté until tender, about 5 minutes. • Stir the mushrooms into the Parmesan sauce. • Preheat the oven to 350°F (180°C/gas 4). • Heat the remaining butter in a medium frying pan over medium heat. Add a ladle of the potato batter and swivel the pan so that it coats the base of the pan. Cook for 3 minutes and then turn the pancake using a pallet knife. Cook until golden brown, 3 minutes. Place pancake on a heated plate and repeat until all the batter is used. • Put one of the pancakes into an oiled ovenproof dish just slightly larger than the pancake. Spread with a layer of the mushroom sauce. Add another pancake and repeat, until all the ingredients are in the pan. Cover with aluminum foil. • Bake for 15 minutes. Remove the foil and bake until lightly browned on top, about 15 minutes. • Serve hot.

1 lb (500 g) starchy (baking) potatoes, peeled
3 large eggs, lightly beaten
1 large egg yolk, lightly beaten
1/2 cup (75 g) all-purpose (plain) flour
Generous 2 1/3 cups (600 ml) milk
Salt and freshly ground black pepper
1/4 cup (60 g) butter
Generous 3/4 cup (100 g) freshly grated Parmesan
2 tablespoons extra-virgin olive oil
12 oz (350 g) white mushrooms, sliced

SERVES 4

PREPARATION 15 min

COOKING 1 h 30 min

DIFFICULTY level 2

# Potato
## and zucchini loaf

Cook the potatoes in a large pot of salted boiling water until tender, 20–25 minutes. • Drain and mash in a large bowl using a potato ricer. • Preheat the oven to 350°F (180°C/gas 4). • Grease a large ovenproof dish. • Heat the oil in a large frying pan over medium heat. Add the onion and garlic and sauté until softened, 3–4 minutes. • Add the zucchini and season with salt and pepper. Sauté for 15 minutes, until the zucchini begin to break down. Remove and discard the garlic. • Add the eggs, Parmesan, and Pecorino to the potato and mix well. • Add the zucchini to the potato mixture and mix well. • Add the parsley and season with salt and pepper. Mix well. • Form the mixture into a large rectangular loaf using your hands. Place the bread crumbs on a work surface and carefully roll the potato loaf in them, coating it evenly. Place in the prepared pan. • Bake for 25 minutes. Turn the loaf and bake until well browned, about 25 minutes. • Slice and serve hot or at room temperature.

1 lb (500 g) starchy (baking) potatoes, peeled
1/4 cup (60 ml) extra-virgin olive oil
1 large onion, finely chopped
1 clove garlic, lightly crushed but whole
1 lb (500 g) zucchini (courgettes), sliced
Salt and freshly ground black pepper
3 large eggs, lightly beaten
1/2 cup (60 g) freshly grated Parmesan
1/2 cup (60 g) freshly grated Pecorino
1 tablespoon finely chopped parsley
1/4 cup (30 g) fine dry bread crumbs

SERVES 4–6

PREPARATION 15 min

COOKING 50 min

DIFFICULTY level 1

# Potato Cakes

## with goat cheese

Preheat the oven to 350°F (180°C/gas 4). • Grease a 6-cup muffin pan. • Put the leaves from a sprig of marjoram in the base of each muffin cup. Add a layer of potato. Add a little cheese and then another layer of potato. Repeat until all the potatoes and cheese are used. Finish with a layer of potato. Dot with butter. Season with salt. • Cover the muffin pan with aluminum foil. • Bake for 40 minutes. Remove the foil. Increase the oven temperature to 400°F (200°C/gas 6). Bake until golden brown, 5–10 more minutes. • Serve hot.

8 small sprigs of marjoram

6 medium starchy (baking) potatoes, peeled and thinly sliced

8 oz (250 g) soft creamy goat cheese

2 tablespoons butter

Salt

SERVES 4

PREPARATION 15 min

COOKING 1 h

DIFFICULTY level 1

# Baked Potatoes

## with bacon and herbs

Preheat the oven to 425°F (220°C/gas 7). • Put the butter into a small bowl. Season with salt and pepper. Add the juniper berries and thyme. Mix well. • Place the butter on a piece of aluminum foil and shape it into a sausage shape using your hands. Wrap it in the foil and chill in the refrigerator. • Wrap the potatoes in aluminum foil and bake until tender, about 1 hour. • Sauté the bacon in a small frying pan over medium heat until crisp, about 5 minutes. • Remove the potatoes from the oven and unwrap them. • Cut open and use the tines of a fork to stir some of the flesh. Season with salt and pepper. • Unwrap the herb butter and slice in four. • Place a slice of herb butter and some cheese and bacon on each potato. Sprinkle with the parsley and serve hot.

½ cup (125 g) butter, softened
Salt and freshly ground black pepper
4 juniper berries, crushed
½ tablespoon finely chopped thyme
4 large starchy (baking) potatoes
4 oz (125 g) bacon, cut into ribbons
8 oz (250 g) Fontina or other tasty firm cheese, grated
2 tablespoons finely chopped parsley

SERVES 4

PREPARATION 15 min

COOKING 40 min

DIFFICULTY level 2

# Potato Frittata
## with ham and peas

Slice 2 of the onions very finely. • Heat 2 tablespoons of the oil in a frying pan over low heat. Add the sliced onions and sauté until they begin to soften, 3–4 minutes. • Add the potatoes and sauté until soft, 10–15 minutes. • Season with salt and pepper. Add the thyme and mix well. Transfer to a bowl and let cool. • Chop the remaining onion. Heat 2 tablespoons of the oil in a frying pan over medium heat. Add the onion and sauté until it begins to soften, 3–4 minutes. • Add the ham and peas. Sauté until the peas are tender, 5–7 minutes. Season with salt and pepper. • Beat the eggs in a bowl. Add the Parmesan and season with salt and pepper. • Pour this mixture over the potatoes and mix well. Add the peas and ham and mix well. • Place the frying pan over medium heat and cook until the egg is almost set, 6–8 minutes. Slide the frittata onto a plate, cover with another plate and flip, then slip it back into the pan. Cook until golden brown, 3–4 minutes. • Serve hot.

3 small onions
1/4 cup (60 ml) extra-virgin olive oil
1 1/2 lb (750 g) waxy (boiling) potatoes, peeled and thinly sliced
Salt and freshly ground black pepper
1 tablespoon finely chopped thyme
3 oz (90 g) ham, chopped
1 1/4 cups (200 g) fresh or frozen peas
4 large eggs
1/2 cup (60 g) freshly grated Parmesan

# Cabbage Roulade
## with potato and cheese filling

SERVES 4

PREPARATION 20 min

COOKING 1 h 35 min

DIFFICULTY level 2

Cook the potatoes in a large pot of salted boiling water until tender, 20–25 minutes. • Drain, return to the pot, and mash until smooth. • Add half the butter and the milk. Cook over low heat, stirring constantly, until the purée is thick and smooth, about 5 minutes. Transfer to a large bowl. • Blanch the cabbage in a large pot of salted boiling water, 3–4 minutes. • Drain well and arrange the leaves, overlapping, on a large piece of muslin, to make a rough rectangle. • Cover with the bacon and sprinkle with the Parmesan. • Melt the remaining butter in a frying pan over medium heat. Add the onion and sauté until softened, 5 minutes. • Add the onion to the potato purée and mix well. Season with salt and pepper. Add the eggs and mix well. • Spoon the potato mixture down the center of the prepared cabbage. Roll up the roulade using the muslin to help you. Wrap the muslin tightly around the roulade and seal the ends, tying securely with kitchen string. • Bring the stock to a boil in a large saucepan over medium heat. Add the roulade and simmer over very low heat for 1 hour. Remove from the heat and let cool slightly. • Remove the roulade from the saucepan and carefully unwrap it. Transfer to a serving dish. Slice the roulade and drizzle it with a little of the stock. Serve hot.

2 lb (1 kg) starchy (baking) potatoes
1/3 cup (90 g) butter
1 cup (250 ml) milk
12 large cabbage leaves
6 oz (180 g) bacon
1/2 cup (60 g) freshly grated Parmesan
2 medium onions, thinly sliced
Salt and freshly ground black pepper
2 large eggs, lightly beaten
8 cups (2 liters) vegetable stock
   (homemade or bouillon cube)

48

SERVES 4

PREPARATION 10 min

COOKING 15–20 min

DIFFICULTY level 1

# Pan Potatoes
## with eggs and scallions

Place the potatoes into a large saucepan and cover with water. Bring to a boil over medium heat. Simmer for 5 minutes. Drain well. • Heat the oil in a large frying pan over medium heat. Add the scallions and potatoes. Sauté for 5 minutes, taking care not to break the potatoes. Season with salt. • Make space around the edges of the pan for the eggs using a spatula. • Break the eggs into the pan and cook until the eggs are set and the potatoes are tender, 5–10 minutes. • Season the eggs with salt. Sprinkle with chile powder and serve hot.

4 large waxy (boiling) potatoes, peeled and thinly sliced
1/4 cup (60 ml) extra-virgin olive oil
6 scallions (green onions), chopped
Salt
4 large eggs
1/4 teaspoon chile powder

# Potato Cakes

## with ham and cheese

Preheat the oven to 350°F ´(180°C/gas 4). • Grease 4 large ramekins. • Arrange a layer of potatoes in the bottom of each ramekin. Add a layer of Fontina and a sliver of garlic to each one. Add a layer of ham. Repeat this layering process until all the ingredients are used. Season with salt and pepper. • Bake for 20 minutes. Remove from the oven and sprinkle with the Gruyère. Bake until the potatoes are tender and browned on top, about 10 more minutes. • Sprinkle with rosemary and serve hot.

6 medium waxy (boiling) potatoes, peeled and thinly sliced

3 oz (90 g) Fontina or other mild firm cheese, sliced thinly

1 clove garlic, very finely sliced

3 oz (90 g) ham, diced

Salt and freshly ground black pepper

1/3 cup (50 g) freshly grated Gruyère cheese

Leaves from 2 sprigs rosemary

SERVES 4

PREPARATION 15 min

COOKING 2 h 15 min

DIFFICULTY level 1

# Baked Potatoes
## with meat sauce

Heat 4 tablespoons of the oil in a large saucepan over medium heat. Add the carrot, celery, and onion. Sauté until softened, 3–4 minutes. • Add the meat and sauté until browned all over, about 5 minutes. • Add the wine and cook until it evaporates, 2–3 minutes. • Add the tomatoes and sage. Mix well, cover, and simmer over very low heat for 2 hours. • Preheat the oven to 400°F (200°C/gas 6). • Arrange the potatoes on an oiled baking sheet and bake until almost tender, about 1 hour. • Cut the potatoes in half lengthwise. Scoop out and discard a little of the potato flesh. • Fill the hollowed out potatoes with the meat sauce. • Place on the baking sheet. Season with salt and pepper. Drizzle with the remaining oil and bake until the potatoes are cooked through, about 5 minutes. • Garnish with the sage and serve hot.

1/3 cup (90 ml) extra-virgin olive oil
1 medium carrot, finely chopped
1 celery stick, finely chopped
1 medium onion, finely chopped
1 lb (500 g) lean ground (minced) beef
1/3 cup (90 ml) red wine
1 (14-oz/400-g) can tomatoes, with juice
3 sage leaves, finely chopped, + whole leaves, to garnish
4 large starchy (baking) potatoes
Salt and freshly ground black pepper

SERVES 4–6

PREPARATION 15 min

COOKING 50 min

DIFFICULTY level 1

# Potato Bake

## with tomatoes and oregano

Preheat the oven to 400°F (200°C/gas 6). • Oil a large ovenproof dish. • Heat 2 tablespoons of the oil in a large frying pan over medium heat. Add the onion and sauté until softened, 4–5 minutes. • Add the potatoes and sauté for 5 minutes. Season with salt and pepper. • Transfer to the ovenproof dish. Arrange the tomatoes in a layer on top of the potatoes. Sprinkle with oregano and bread crumbs. Drizzle with the remaining oil. • Bake until the potatoes are tender, 35–40 minutes. • Serve hot.

$1/3$ cup (90 ml) extra-virgin olive oil
1 large onion, finely chopped
$1^1/2$ lb (750 g) potatoes, peeled and thinly sliced
Salt and freshly ground black pepper
12 oz (350 g) cherry tomatoes, halved
$1/2$ teaspoon dried oregano
$1/2$ cup (60 g) fine dry bread crumbs

# Sweet Potato
## stew with onions

Sauté the onions and garlic in the oil in a large frying pan over medium heat until lightly browned, about 5 minutes. • Add the paprika, cayenne pepper, and tomato purèe. • Stir in the sweet potatoes and cook for 1 minute. • Pour in ½ cup (125 ml) of wine and the water and bring to a boil. Cover and simmer over low heat until the sauce has thickened, about 10 minutes. • Season with salt and pepper. Pour in the remaining wine. • Cover and cook until the sweet potatoes are tender, 10–15 minutes. • Serve hot.

2 large red onions, finely chopped
2 cloves garlic, finely chopped
3 tablespoons extra-virgin olive oil
1 tablespoon sweet paprika
1 teaspoon cayenne pepper
1 tablespoon tomato purèe (paste)
3 lb (1.5 kg) sweet potatoes, peeled and quartered
1 cup (250 ml) dry white wine
1 cup (250 ml) water
Salt and freshly ground black pepper

SERVES 4

PREPARATION 15 min

COOKING 45–50 min

DIFFICULTY level 1

# Potato Cakes
## with sautéed cherry tomatoes

Preheat the oven to 350°F (180°C/gas 4). • Oil 6 large ramekins. • Cook the potatoes in a large pot of salted boiling water until tender, 15–20 minutes. • Drain and mash using a potato ricer. Place in a large bowl. • Add the ham and shallots. Season with salt and pepper and mix well. • Beat the eggs in a bowl. Add the beaten eggs to the potato mixture and mix well. • Divide the potato mixture among the prepared ramekins. • Bake until lightly browned, about 20 minutes. • While the potato cakes are in the oven, heat the oil in a medium frying pan over medium heat. Add the tomatoes and thyme. Season with salt and pepper and sauté for 5 minutes. Remove from the heat. • Remove the potato cakes from the oven and turn out onto a heated serving dish. • Spoon the tomato mixture over the top. • Serve hot.

1½ lb (750 g) starchy (baking) potatoes, peeled and cut into chunks

4 oz (125 g) ham, chopped

2 shallots, finely chopped

Salt and freshly ground black pepper

4 large eggs

¼ cup (60 ml) extra-virgin olive oil

1½ lb (750 g) cherry tomatoes, cut in half

1 tablespoon finely chopped of thyme

SERVES 4

PREPARATION 25 min

COOKING 1 h 25 min

DIFFICULTY level 2

# Potato Croquettes
## with mushroom filling

Preheat the oven to 350°F (180°C/gas 4). • Bake the potatoes until tender, 50–55 minutes. • Remove from the oven and let cool slightly. Peel and purée using a potato ricer. • Oil a large ovenproof dish. Increase the oven temperature to 400°F (200°C/gas 6). • Heat the oil in a large frying pan over medium heat. Add the garlic and sauté until pale golden brown, 3–4 minutes. • Add the mushrooms, lower the heat, cover, and simmer until the mushrooms are tender, 5–10 minutes. • Add the thyme and season with salt. • Mix the potato purée, eggs, and flour in a large bowl. Form the mixture into balls the size of large walnuts. Press a spoonful of the mushroom mixture into the center of each one and cover with the potato, ensuring that the mushroom filling is well sealed. • Place the bread crumbs on a plate. Roll the croquettes in the bread crumbs. • Arrange the croquettes in the prepared dish and bake until well browned, 20–25 minutes. • Serve hot.

1½ lb (750 g) starchy (baking) potatoes
2 tablespoons extra-virgin olive oil
1 clove garlic, lightly crushed but whole
12 oz (350 g) mixed frozen mushrooms, chopped
2 tablespoons finely chopped thyme
Salt
2 large eggs, lightly beaten
¼ cup (30 g) all-purpose (plain) flour
1 cup (125 g) fine dry bread crumbs

**60**

# Potato Fritters

Cook the potatoes in a large pot of salted boiling water until tender, 20–25 minutes. • Drain and purée using a potato ricer. • Bring the water and butter to a boil in a medium saucepan over medium heat. Add the flour and mix well to prevent lumps forming. Cook for 3 minutes, stirring constantly, until the mixture comes away from the sides of the pan. Remove from the heat. • Add 1 of the eggs and mix well. Add the remaining eggs one at a time, mixing well after each addition. • Stir in the potato and season with salt and pepper. • Heat the oil in a deep-fryer or large frying pan over medium heat. Drop in spoonfuls of the batter and fry until golden brown, about 5 minutes each batch. • Remove with a slotted spoon and drain on paper towels. • Sprinkle with salt and serve hot.

12 oz (350 g) starchy (baking) potatoes, peeled
1 cup (250 ml) water
1/4 cup (60 g) butter
3/4 cup (125 g) all-purpose (plain) flour
3 large eggs, lightly beaten
Salt and freshly ground black pepper
3 cups (750 ml) olive oil, for frying

**SERVES** 4–6

**PREPARATION** 10 min + 1 h to rise

**COOKING** 35 min

**DIFFICULTY** level 2

# Potato Focaccia

## with rosemary

Cook the potatoes in a large pot of salted boiling water until tender, 20–25 minutes. • Drain and purée in a large bowl using a potato ricer. • Mix the yeast and water in a small bowl. • Put the flour into a large bowl with a pinch of salt and the extra-virgin olive oil. Mix well. Add the yeast solution and mix to make a dough. • Add the potatoes and mix well with a wooden spoon. • Cover and let rise for 1 hour. • Turn the dough out onto a lightly floured work surface and knead for 2 minutes. • Divide the dough into 8 portions and flatten each one slightly with your hand. • Heat the peanut oil in a large frying pan over medium heat. • Fry the potato focaccias for 2–3 minutes. Turn using a spatula and fry until golden brown all over, 2–3 minutes more. • Remove with a slotted spoon and drain on paper towels. • Sprinkle with salt and rosemary and serve hot.

12 oz (350 g) starchy (baking) potatoes, peeled

1 oz (30 g) fresh yeast or 2 ($\frac{1}{4}$-oz/7-g) packages active dry yeast

$\frac{1}{3}$ cup (90 ml) lukewarm water

1$\frac{1}{3}$ cups (200 g) all-purpose (plain) flour

Salt

2 tablespoons extra-virgin olive oil

$\frac{1}{2}$ cup (125 ml) peanut oil, for frying

2 tablespoons finely chopped rosemary

# Index

*Potatoes*

was created and produced by McRae Books Srl

Borgo Santa Croce, 8 – Florence (Italy)

info@mcraebooks.com

Publishers: Anne McRae and Marco Nardi

Project Director: Anne McRae

Design: Sara Mathews

Text: Carla Bardi

Editing: Osla Fraser

Photography: Mauro Corsi, Leonardo Pasquinelli, Gianni Petronio, Lorenzo Borri, Stefano Pratesi

Home Economist: Benedetto Rillo

Artbuying: McRae Books

Layouts: Adina Stefania Dragomir

Repro: Fotolito Raf, Florence

ISBN 978-88-89272-88-6

Printed and bound in China